SCHOLASTIC

STANDARDS-BASED

SCIENCE

LEARNING CENTERS

by Lynne Kepler

NEW YORK • TORONTO • LONDON • AUCKLAND • SYDNEY **Teaching**
MEXICO CITY • NEW DELHI • HONG KONG • BUENOS AIRES *Resources*

Dedication

To Doug, Jake, Ty, and Muir Linnaea

Acknowledgments

My warmest thanks to the following folks for "touching" this book in some way: editor Joan Novelli, who has shepherded my writing endeavors; Dr. Carl Callenbach, who helped me discover the child-centered classroom; my husband Doug and our three children who inspire and motivate all my science experiences; and to the teachers (friends and acquaintances) who demonstrate the impact "doing science" has on children.

Cover design by Jason Robinson
Interior design by Jason Robinson and Holly Grundon
Cover illustrations by Rick Brown
Illustrations by Jeffrey Wiener

ISBN 0-439-79280-0
Copyright © 1995 by Lynne Kepler
All rights reserved.
Printed in the U.S.A.

6 7 8 9 10   40   12

Table of Contents

From the Author

You know the old saying, "Seeing is believing." Well, I was fortunate early in my teaching career to be part of a classroom that was organized around learning centers. What I saw was a bunch of six- and seven-year-olds who were full of questions and who showed me how learning centers could be manageable and still full of excitement. From that time on, I was convinced that centers and a child-centered approach to teaching make a great fit.

A couple of years later, I had my eyes opened again—this time to the wonder that science brings to our lives. I met my husband—and my educational philosophy met science. His interest in science was contagious. I learned that I really loved science. But more importantly, I learned that kids love science, too. Bringing science into the classroom allows children to explore their world and encourages them to make meaningful connections as they learn—connections that will assist them throughout their lives.

Put science and centers together and the result is learning that is exciting and meaningful. Set up science centers in you classroom and you'll see kids discovering, drawing, thinking, writing, observing, experimenting, sharing—all part of the work of scientists. Seeing is believing!

— *Lynne Kepler*

Setting Up Your Science Centers

This book is an invitation to you and your students. An invitation to classroom spaces and places where students can explore their world and learn by doing—a place where students make observations, ask questions, investigate predictions, reflect on their discoveries, and form conclusions. A space where learning is exciting and fun. Welcome to science centers!

How do you develop a science center? This book will guide you on that journey. But first, here are a few things to keep in mind before you begin:

◐ Learning centers—science or otherwise—can support any teaching style, including yours! The trick is in doing what feels most comfortable to you—and that process of finding a good fit usually takes a bit of experimenting. Some teachers find that beginning small and then expanding the size and number of their centers is the most manageable approach. Each of the centers in this book is easy to set up and get going. Just choose one that connects with your curriculum or has special appeal to you and your students.

◐ Remember that the center designs and activities in this book are suggestions only. If they spark ideas in your classroom, all the better. As long as children are engaged, there are no rules for how a learning center should look or what it should contain. But in case you want a little help in the design department, each center in this book comes complete with illustrated tips for setting up a special place for learning—one that is as much fun to be at as it is a great place to explore and learn.

◐ In addition to using the student assessment strategies cited in each center, consider using kid-watching techniques to assess how well your centers are working. Take time to just sit and observe your students at work. Take notes, too. Are students interested and engaged? Do they appear to know what to do? Are they making productive use of their time at the center? If not, can you tell why not? Invite students to share what they liked and didn't like about any one center or center activity for extra insights into how you can make improvements. Be prepared to adjust your center setups and content.

What Can a Science Center Add to Your Classroom?

Including a science center in your classroom demonstrates to your students the important role that science plays in our everyday lives. It is a strategy that provides young children with time and space to manipulate and explore materials, make observations, and solve problems. It has been well documented that children who are actually doing science will learn more skills and concepts than those who are in traditional text-based science programs.

A science center helps you provide other opportunities for students, including:

o working in small, cooperative groups;

o a location for ongoing, longer-term investigations;

o effective use of materials (you may not need as many or as much);

o making connections among curricular areas.

What Does a Science Center Look Like?

Touchable! A science center that is inviting and reflects the work and personalities of your students is one that will draw students in again and again. Whatever the topic, you'll want to be sure to include:

o objects of general interest, such as plants and animals;

o tools of the trade, such as magnifying lenses, prisms, and writing materials;

o books on topics related to center activities; and

o lots of student-generated work, such as illustrations, graphs, and charts.

Tips for Getting Organized, Setting Up, and Managing Your Centers

As Michael Opitz says in his book *Learning Centers: Getting Them Started... Keeping Them Going* (Scholastic, 1994), "In learning-centered classrooms especially, management is critical because students move around the room and learn to take more responsibility for their learning. Without a plan, chaos is certain." Here then are some tried-and-true organizational and management strategies.

Plot and Plan

Organize your room to accommodate your centers and other classroom needs (such as a whole-class meeting space). Begin by making a map of your room. Note the fixed features (windows, doors, outlets) and make a separate list of any moveable furniture. Make a list of your room needs and intentions, including notations such as: *want three learning center areas*; *science center must be near a window and a bulletin board*; *art center should be near the sink*; and so on. Then sketch furniture in place on the map so you can create cozy corners, accommodate traffic patterns, allow for student storage, and so on. Revise until you're satisfied.

When deciding on a spot for your science center, think about all the science happening outside your window—weather, plant growth, animal life, seasons—you'll see why a spot near a window is the perfect place for a science center. Provide room to display student work, charts, and posters.

Try to arrange a worktable and a few chairs nearby, and make room on shelves (or set up temporary shelving with boards and bricks) for storage space. Try storing additional materials in cardboard file boxes, shoe boxes, baskets, and resealable plastic bags.

Map Out Management

After introducing students to a center and generating a list of guidelines together, let them role-play how to use the center. Post a schedule (you might color code the groups) and let students practice making rounds. For example, if you set up a rotation schedule in which small groups work at the center at different times during the day (or on different days), have students run through the procedure so everyone understands how the center schedule works.

Encourage students to recognize that while they are returning from or going to the center, the rest of the class may be hard at work on something else. Develop a simple signal or code word to remind overly exuberant students to bring down the noise level.

If you have additional centers operating in your classroom, consider opening the centers one at a time to reduce confusion. Begin with one center. Then, once students are comfortable with the routine and demonstrate sufficient independence, introduce a second center.

Stock Up and Set Up

Each center has a materials list all its own, but you can plan ahead to collect the items on this suggested list of generic supplies:

- scissors
- markers
- paper towels
- resealable plastic bags
- white copy paper
- scrap paper
- construction paper

- paste and glue sticks
- pencils
- chart paper
- clear tape
- hand lenses
- crayons
- heavy white paper

Let students help bring each center to life. Invite them to create signs for centers, brainstorm guidelines for working at the center, and contribute collected treasures for study (rocks that glitter, tree bark chewed by beaver, feathers, and so on). Students can devise ways to showcase their collectibles. For example, they might construct mini-museum exhibits for shells and other tiny treasures by lining shoe boxes with felt and using cardboard strips to make individual display sections.

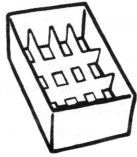

What Are Some Ways to Assess Students' Progress?

In addition to the kid-watching assessment techniques mentioned earlier, you'll want to employ the strategies for assessment included with each center in this book. To keep track of student progress at the centers, have each student maintain a Science Center File Folder to hold work in progress and finished work. Students can use markers to decorate their folders, or collect samples from outdoors and preserve them on their folders under square patches of clear adhesive paper. They may also decide to add just one icon representing each center explored from this book to the cover of their folder (an animal track, a handprint, and so on). Provide a box at the center to store folders.

Remember, we learn best what we enjoy. So add your own ideas—and those of your students—to the ones you find here. Together, you can create centers that invite active learning all year long.

All About Me

What's something each of your students has that no one else has? As they work at this center, students will be delighted to discover that their fingerprints are uniquely theirs! This center is perfect for helping students learn more about themselves and for introducing students to each other, to you, and to science centers!

Science Standards

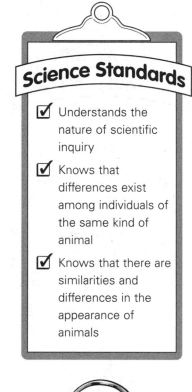

☑ Understands the nature of scientific inquiry

☑ Knows that differences exist among individuals of the same kind of animal

☑ Knows that there are similarities and differences in the appearance of animals

Materials

○ light, brightly colored craft paper
○ student photos (at least two of each child)
○ packing tape or wall adhesive
○ scissors
○ washable-ink pads
○ fine-line markers

Skills

observing, classifying, comparing, communicating, collecting and recording data, inferring, interpreting

Decorating the Center

Cut out a wallpaper-size border strip and tape it to a wall space near the center. Attach photos or self-portraits of students, leaving room for handprints between each photo. Have students press their hands and thumbs into an ink pad and then on the paper to make handprints and thumbprints directly on the wall border.

Getting Started

On a piece of chart paper, illustrate and label each of the three different fingerprint types to create a graph. Display this chart at the center. (Students will use the chart to graph class fingerprint types by placing their left thumbprints in the appropriate column.)

Introducing the Center

Before students work at the center, meet with the whole class to brainstorm ways they are alike and ways they are different. Record responses on a chart and display at the center.

Teaching Tip

Before students try this activity, you may want to demonstrate the finger-printing procedure (see student directions).

Materials

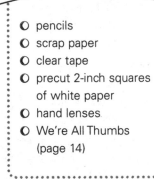

- ○ pencils
- ○ scrap paper
- ○ clear tape
- ○ precut 2-inch squares of white paper
- ○ hand lenses
- ○ We're All Thumbs (page 14)

Math Connection

Use thumbprint graphs to practice math skills like counting, ordering, and addition. Ask students: *How many fingerprints match the arch pattern? the whorl? the loop? Which fingerprint pattern is most common in our class?* Go further to look at handedness. Students can count, record, and compare the number of left-handed and right-handed classmates.

You Are Thum-body Special

Student Directions

Copy & Post

1. Make a dark, smudgy mark with a pencil on a sheet of paper.

2. Rub your thumb in the smudge, covering your entire thumbprint.

3. Place a piece of clear tape over the smudgy thumb.

4. Remove the tape from your thumb and put it on a square of paper.

5. Use a hand lens to look at your thumbprint.

6. Compare your thumbprint with a friend's thumbprint. How are they different? How are they alike?

7. Find the pattern that looks like your thumbprint on the chart. Paste your thumbprint in this row.

8. Fill in your "We're All Thumbs" graph.

Activity #2

Teaching Tip

Zebras' stripes, like our fingerprints, are unique. Each zebra has its own stripe pattern. This activity helps students explore the concept of same and different—and invites discussion about similarities and differences among themselves.

Materials

- precut 5-inch squares of heavy stock white paper
- white crayons
- cups of water
- paintbrushes
- black watercolor paint
- Zebra Cutouts (page 14)

Zany Zebra Prints

Copy & Post

Student Directions

1. Write your name on one side of a piece of paper. On the other side, draw a stripe pattern over the whole area with a white crayon.

2. Paint over the whole paper with black watercolor paint. Let dry.

3. After your paper is dry, turn it over. Use a Zebra Cutout to trace a zebra on the blank side of the paper. Cut it out.

ABC

Vocabulary Connection

As students finish their prints, surround the fingerprint chart with this herd of zany zebras! Invite students to compare the zebras. Questions to sharpen both descriptive language and observation skills include: *Can you find wavy stripes? straight stripes? wiggly stripes? What other words describe stripes you see? What words could you use to describe the shades of black and white?*

Extension

Use this activity as a springboard to discussing likenesses and differences among students. For example, you might invite students to sort themselves by shirts (patterns/no patterns or stripes/no stripes), by hair (wavy/straight/curly), and so on. Conclude by asking children what qualities and characteristics they share.

Activity #3

Helping Hands

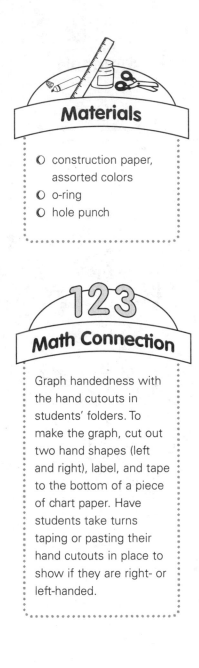

Materials

- construction paper, assorted colors
- o-ring
- hole punch

123
Math Connection

Graph handedness with the hand cutouts in students' folders. To make the graph, cut out two hand shapes (left and right), label, and tape to the bottom of a piece of chart paper. Have students take turns taping or pasting their hand cutouts in place to show if they are right- or left-handed.

Student Directions

Copy & Post

1. Compare your hands with a friend's hands. How are they similar? different?

2. Trace both of your hands on a piece of colored paper.

LEFT   RIGHT

3. Cut out the hands. Write your name on both hands.

4. Write left on the left-hand cutout and right on the right-hand cutout.

5. Find the hand cutout that matches the hand you use to hold a crayon. Put this hand in your science work folder.

6. Think about the kinds of things your hands help you do. Write one of these things on the other hand cutout. (Note to teachers: Younger children can dictate their helping-hands ideas.)

Literature Connection

Make a hand-shaped book by punching holes in students' remaining hand cutouts (the ones they have written helping ideas on). Join hand shapes together with an o-ring. Display in a handy science-center location for students to read. Help students put their pictures together to create a border or other display at the science center. Invite students to read their own pages to parents at your next conference day or open house.

Center Assessment Tip

Create a simple chart that students can complete with a classmate.
The chart could look like this:

Names _____ _____	
How We Are Alike	**How We Are Different**

Have students complete the chart by listing several ways they are
alike and several ways they are different.

• •

Related Children's Books

Hanimations by Mario Mariotti (Kane Miller, 1998). A wondrous array
of animals, real and imagined, all created from the painted hands of
the author and his daughter.

The Kissing Hand by Audrey Penn (Child & Family Press, 1993).
Chester Raccoon's mother shares with him a special family secret—
the Kissing Hand—to comfort him while he's away at school.

Thumbprints Circus by Rodney Peppe (Yearling, 1992). Illustrations
created with thumbprints invite children to explore fingerprints.

We're All Thumbs!

Color in the number of blocks that show how many thumbprints in your class are arches, loops, or whorls. Use a different color for each fingerprint type.

Arches	Loops	Whorls
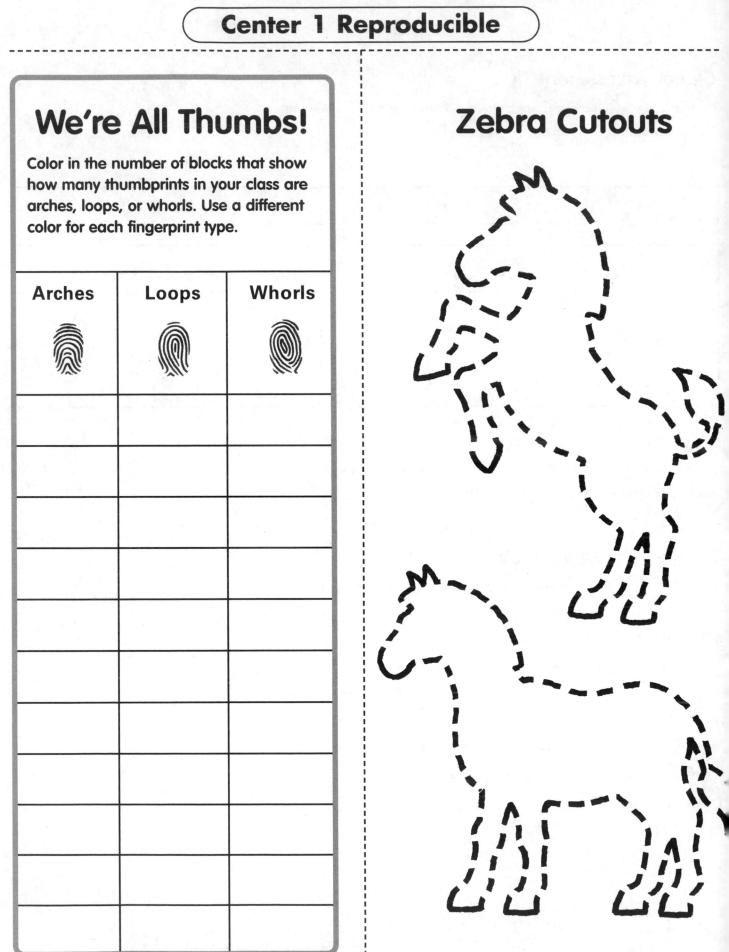		

Zebra Cutouts

Eye Spy

At this center, students will look at the world in a whole new way. What do students know about their own eyes? About animal eyes? Children will observe eye colors found in their class, collect and compare pictures of animals' eyes, and construct eyeglasses that simulate the way a worm sees the world.

Design Tip
Make a peek-through fence designed to invite visual investigations.

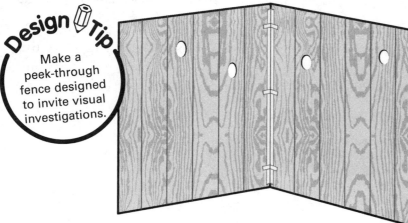

Materials

- large pieces of cardboard (the sides of appliance boxes are perfect)
- craft knife (adult use only)
- brown marker
- yardstick or meterstick
- packing tape

Decorating the Center

Use a craft knife to cut or score the cardboard into a series of sections representing fence slats (at least 1-inch wide and approximately 3 to 4 feet high). Place tape lengthwise to join or reinforce section joints. Add a few pieces of tape horizontally to strengthen joint hinges. Add lines and knotholes with markers to give the appearance of a wooden fence. Cut out circles in the center of several knotholes so students can peep through the fence.

Add a sign to your fence reading "What Do Your Eyes Spy?" Change the scenery behind the fence periodically. For example, tape "mystery pictures" behind each hole and challenge students to guess what the pictures show from the portion they can see through the fence hole. Another time, tape bits of colored cellophane behind each hole.

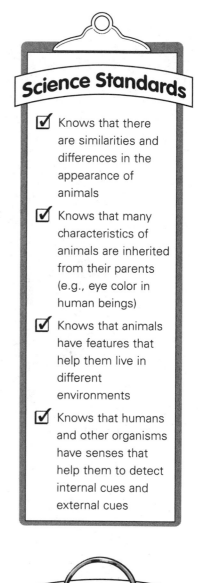

Science Standards

- ☑ Knows that there are similarities and differences in the appearance of animals
- ☑ Knows that many characteristics of animals are inherited from their parents (e.g., eye color in human beings)
- ☑ Knows that animals have features that help them live in different environments
- ☑ Knows that humans and other organisms have senses that help them to detect internal cues and external cues

Skills

observing, comparing, classifying, communicating, collecting and recording data, making models, interpreting

Getting Started

Hang a mirror at the center for students who may want to take a closer look at their own eyes. Make and display an eye-color graph on a large piece of chart paper. Invite students to suggest eye colors to graph. Create one column for each color with at least 20 blocks in each column. Hang the graph in the center for students to complete as part of Activity 1 (Look Into My Eyes).

Introducing the Center

Give each student a copy of the My Eyes reproducible (page 19). As a pre-center activity, have students complete the page to show what they already know about eyes. Have students keep these in their science work folders until the end of the center, at which time they can make any changes they feel they need to make.

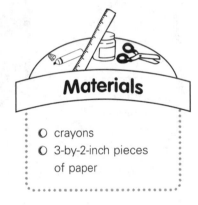

Materials

- ◯ crayons
- ◯ 3-by-2-inch pieces of paper

Math Connection

Have students use the information from the eye-color graph to write or dictate their own word problems. Put word problems together in a bag or box and let students randomly select problems to solve.

Activity #1

Look Into My Eyes

Student Directions

Copy & Post

1. Sit back-to-back with a classmate. Guess each other's eye color. Tell each other your guesses.

2. Turn around and look at each other's eyes.

3. On a piece of paper, draw your partner's eyes. Use crayon or marker to show the color. Write your partner's name.

4. Paste your eye-color papers on the eye-color graph.

Activity #2

Getting Started

Display precut pictures of animals at the center. You might tape them to the fence along the bottom, paste them to posterboard, or laminate and display them at the table.

Mystery Eyes

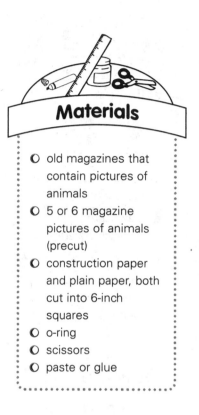

Copy & Post

Student Directions

1. Look through the peepholes. Do you see the same thing through each hole?

2. Look at the animal pictures. How are their eyes like yours? How are they different?

3. Look through the magazines for pictures of animals. Cut out one animal picture. Paste it to a piece of paper. Write the name of the animal in the bottom right corner of the page. Write your name in the top right corner.

4. Place a piece of construction paper on top of your picture. Cut out a circle from the part of the construction paper that covers the eyes of the animal.

5. Paste the two sheets of paper together along the left edge.

6. Share your animal-eyes picture with a friend. Can your friend guess what animal these eyes belong to?

Materials

- ○ old magazines that contain pictures of animals
- ○ 5 or 6 magazine pictures of animals (precut)
- ○ construction paper and plain paper, both cut into 6-inch squares
- ○ o-ring
- ○ scissors
- ○ paste or glue

Follow-up

Collect students' animal-eyes pictures and compile into a class "Animal Eye Peek-a-Boo" book. Punch a hole in the top left corner of each picture and put them all together with an o-ring. Display at the science center.

Worm Glasses

Copy & Post

Student Directions

1. Trace the eyeglass pattern on a file-folder piece. Cut out the eyeglasses.

2. Paste wax-paper squares inside the glasses. Put on your worm glasses.

3. Have a friend empty the paper bag.

4. Pick up any ten pieces of cloth.

5. With your glasses on, tell how many of each color you chose.

6. Take off your glasses. Now look at the colors you really picked up. Record your results on the "When I Was a Worm..." sheet. Try this activity again. Compare results.

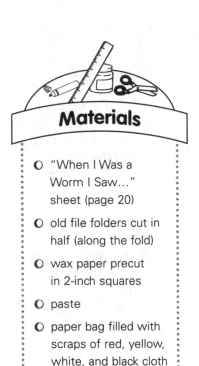

Materials

- ○ "When I Was a Worm I Saw..." sheet (page 20)
- ○ old file folders cut in half (along the fold)
- ○ wax paper precut in 2-inch squares
- ○ paste
- ○ paper bag filled with scraps of red, yellow, white, and black cloth

Follow-up

The wax paper cuts down on the amount of light transmitted to the eye; therefore, it affects ability to distinguish between colors. Worms are similarly able to see only certain ranges.

Center Assessment Tip

Have students review the "My Eyes..." reproducible they completed in the center introduction activity. Then invite them to make changes to their sheets to show what they learned.

Related Children's Books

Arthur's Eyes by Marc Brown (Little Brown, 1986). A pair of glasses helps this favorite aardvark solve some problems.

How Animals See Things by Allan Fowler (Children's Press, 1999). Colorful photographs give kids a glimpse of animals' sense of sight.

Name _____

My Eyes . . .

My eyes look like this:	My eyes can see
	_____ _____ _____ _____ _____
My eyes are the same color as a _____ ; as _____ 's eyes; as _____ .	**My eyes are different from** _____ 's eyes because _____ .

Name _____

When I was a worm I saw . . .

Try 1	Try 2
_____ red	_____ red
_____ white	_____ white
_____ yellow	_____ yellow
_____ black	_____ black

Pumpkin Life Cycle

How does a pumpkin change after it becomes a jack-o'-lantern? The activities in this center will help students answer this question as they investigate the pumpkin plant's life cycle, including decomposition and germination. Students record observations and discoveries in pumpkin diaries.

Design Tip

Grow a bulletin-board pumpkin patch designed to hold students' pumpkin diaries. Here's how:

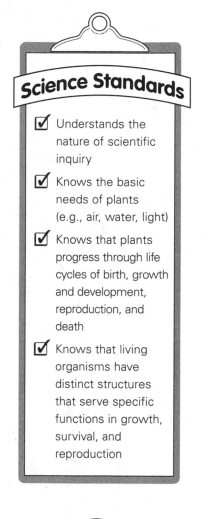

Science Standards

☑ Understands the nature of scientific inquiry

☑ Knows the basic needs of plants (e.g., air, water, light)

☑ Knows that plants progress through life cycles of birth, growth and development, reproduction, and death

☑ Knows that living organisms have distinct structures that serve specific functions in growth, survival, and reproduction

Materials

○ blue and brown craft paper
○ orange construction paper
○ thumbtacks

○ markers
○ scissors
○ tray

○ stapler
○ pumpkin

Skills

observing, predicting, measuring, communicating

Decorating the Center

Cover a bulletin board with blue craft paper. Cover the bottom half in brown craft paper. Tear the top edge of the brown paper so it is slightly uneven. Cut the orange construction paper into pumpkin-shaped diary covers. "Plant" the pumpkins in the patch using the thumbtacks. Add patch details such as vines and leaves. Have students pick their pumpkin covers and add eight pumpkin pages (see page 25) to make diaries. Students can return diaries to the pumpkin patch when not in use.

Getting Started

Set the pumpkin on a tray to make it easier for children to move it around while working. If you made the folding cardboard screen/fence for Center 2 (page 15), use it to display students' jack-o'-lantern pictures (see Activity 3, page 23).

Introducing the Center

Brainstorm words that describe the pumpkin. Record these words on a large pumpkin-shaped chart and display at the center. Share a sample pumpkin diary. Explain that students will make their own diaries at the center and will use them to record observations and thoughts about the pumpkin's life. Encourage students to refer to the chart for spelling and word-choice help as they write in their pumpkin diaries.

Activity #1

Getting Started

Prepare master copies of diary pages by making two copies of the pumpkin page reproducible and adding the following writing and drawing prompts, one per page: (1) *This is what our pumpkin looks like.* (2) *Words that describe our pumpkin.* (3) *I think the pumpkin's inside looks like this.* (4) *Trace some pumpkin seeds here.* (5) *This is what I think will happen to the seeds.* (6) *This is what the inside really looks like.* (7) *Words that describe the inside.* (8) *This is what the pumpkin looks like after one week.* Copy a set for each student.

Pumpkin Close-Up

Copy & Post

Student Directions

1. Cut apart the Pumpkin Diary Pages. Place inside pumpkin covers. Staple together to make a diary.

2. Look at the pumpkin. Draw a picture of the pumpkin on page 1 of your diary.

3. What words describe your pumpkin? Write these words on page 2.

4. What do you think the pumpkin looks like on the inside? Draw a picture on page 3.

5. Put your diary in your science work folder when you are finished.

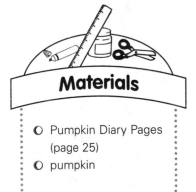

Materials

- Pumpkin Diary Pages (page 25)
- pumpkin

Activity #2

What's the Scoop?

Copy & Post

Student Directions

1. Scoop out one spoonful from the inside of the pumpkin.

2. Put five pumpkin seeds in the bowl.

3. Complete pages 4, 5, 6, and 7 in your diary.

4. After one week, complete page 8.

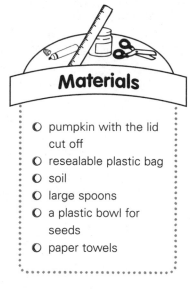

Materials

- O pumpkin with the lid cut off
- O resealable plastic bag
- O soil
- O large spoons
- O a plastic bowl for seeds
- O paper towels

Note to Teachers

For Activity 2, the lid comes off the pumpkin. This activity will be set up for one day only. At the end of the day, set the seeds aside to dry for use in the last center activity. Plan on concluding the day by turning the pumpkin into a jack-o'-lantern. Save the pieces you cut out, some seeds intact, in a resealable plastic sandwich bag that has an inch of soil in the bottom. Keep the contents of the bag moist. Display in the center so the students can record their observations in their diaries. In about one week, students will begin to notice mold growing on the pumpkin pieces.

Activity #3

Feelings on Faces

Copy & Post

Student Directions

1. Think about the ways faces can show feelings.

2. Draw a jack-o'-lantern with a face that shows a feeling. Color and cut out.

3. Tape your jack-o'-lantern to a craft stick.

4. Ask a few classmates to put on a pumpkin puppet show with you.

5. Tape your pumpkins to the cardboard fence at the center.

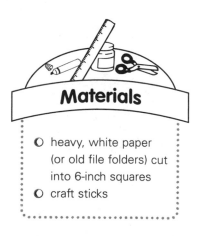

Materials

- O heavy, white paper (or old file folders) cut into 6-inch squares
- O craft sticks

Follow-up

After all students have added their pumpkins to the display, take a tour. Invite students to guess the different expressions. Talk about ways students show their own feelings.

Activity #4

The Pumpkin Cycle

Copy & Post

Student Directions

1. Fold one of the paper towels into a square.

2. Press a wet sponge on the paper towel.

3. Put the paper towel inside the plastic bag.

4. Put five pumpkin seeds on the paper towel. Close the bag.

5. Write your name on the bag with the marker. Place in a sunny spot.

6. Draw or write in your diary on page 7.

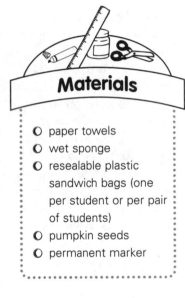

Materials

○ paper towels
○ wet sponge
○ resealable plastic sandwich bags (one per student or per pair of students)
○ pumpkin seeds
○ permanent marker

Center Assessment Tip

Ask each child to share diary entries at a brief individual conference.

Related Children's Books

These books depict the various stages of a pumpkin's life cycle:

The Pumpkin Book by Gail Gibbons (Holiday House, 2000)

Pumpkin, Pumpkin by Jeanne Titherington (HarperTrophy, 1990)

Pumpkin Diary Pages

Date _____

Date _____

Date _____

Date _____

Window Watch

Transform a classroom window into an exciting look-and-see center that will spark science investigations all year long. From wind and weather to bird migration, the options are wide open. If you don't have a window in your classroom, adopt one. Check out the possibilities around the school building and decide on the most feasible option. With a few simple setups, your window will open for business!

Design Tip

Have students help you create a personalized window treatment for this center. Here's how:

Materials

- drawing paper or poster board
- fabric crayons
- two twin-size, light-colored bedsheets
- iron (adult use only)
- puff paints (optional)
- blank calendar grid

Decorating the Center

Have students use fabric crayons to draw pictures of themselves. Demonstrate how to draw a window around the pictures so it appears that they are looking through a window (or, just draw a window on a piece of standard-size paper, make a copy for each child, and have them draw their pictures directly on the windows, tracing the window outline with fabric crayon, too). Iron window drawings on sheets (or drapery-size sheets of butcher paper), following directions on the crayon box. Students can use puff paints to trace details on their drawings. Hang panels of decorated sheets from the top of your window and staple in place. Create a rainbow-shaped sign reading: "Look through our window... What do you see?" Tack in place to connect the drapes.

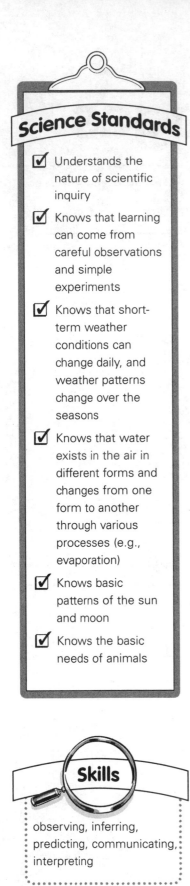

Science Standards

- ☑ Understands the nature of scientific inquiry
- ☑ Knows that learning can come from careful observations and simple experiments
- ☑ Knows that short-term weather conditions can change daily, and weather patterns change over the seasons
- ☑ Knows that water exists in the air in different forms and changes from one form to another through various processes (e.g., evaporation)
- ☑ Knows basic patterns of the sun and moon
- ☑ Knows the basic needs of animals

Skills

observing, inferring, predicting, communicating, interpreting

Getting Started

Sample Window Watch investigations are provided in the following section. Consider selecting a new investigation each month. At the beginning of the month, give each student a copy of a blank calendar grid. (First make a master, writing in the new investigation topic or question.)

Students can record their findings as many times as they visit the center each month, keeping the activity sheet in their science folders. At the end of the month, hold a whole-class sharing session to discuss their findings. Compile and record students' findings on a fresh activity sheet and add to a Window Watch notebook that you keep on the windowsill.

• •

Window Watch Investigations

What's happening outside your window? Add your own and your students' ideas to those here. Let students take turns selecting the topic of the month. Or select to make seasonable or curriculum connections.

Seasons

Look out the window. How can you tell it is (fill in the season)? Students note seasonal changes like leaf color, outerwear, precipitation, and so on.

• •

Temperature

What is the temperature outside? What are your clues? Students can keep ongoing records of temperature trends. Work together to translate into a class bar graph.

• •

Clouds

What do clouds tell us about the weather? Have students illustrate types of clouds and note weather conditions. At the end of the month, look for a correlation between clouds and weather.

Birds

What kind of birds live around the schoolyard? Students work in groups to place simple feeder trays outside the windows. They can observe the kinds of birds at the feeder, the times of day they see them, and so on.

Night Sky

Can you see the moon only at night? During certain days of the lunar cycle, students will be able to see the moon in the morning or in the afternoon. They can illustrate the phase seen and note the date.

Puddles

Where does water in a puddle go when the puddle dries up? Have students work in groups to come up with an explanation of where the water goes. Then have each group fill two clear, plastic cups with water, mark the water line on each cup, then cover one cup with plastic wrap and secure with a rubber band. Leave the other cup open. Students can record observations on the reproducible.

Shapes

What shapes can you spot outside your window? Students can look for a certain shape each day or week, or you can decorate the edges of the activity sheet to suggest shapes they might spot. Students might look for shapes in nature, in other buildings, and so on. Repeat the activity, substituting patterns for shapes.

Tracks Tell Tales

Like a good book, the tracks animals leave behind can tell some fascinating tales. The activities at this center will involve students in observing different kinds of tracks made by animals. Students will use what they learn to create their own track tales.

Design Tip
Create a trail of tracks to lead the way to this center.

Materials

- white chalk
- black construction paper
- scissors
- copy paper
- wide, clear packing tape or wall adhesive
- overhead projector (optional)
- resource containing animal-track patterns (see page 32)

Decorating the Center

Use the chalk to trace a variety of animal tracks onto the black paper (see page 31). Or use copy paper to trace tracks from resources and then use the overhead projector to enlarge shapes before cutting them out. For each animal species represented, make several sets of tracks. Fun tracks to try include bear, duck, fox, moose, and frog. Tape down a trail of tracks leading from the classroom door to the center. Also tape sets of tracks moving up and around the door, across the walls, over the desks, and so on.

Teaching Tip

If you place tape so it covers each track, you will automatically laminate the track in place. Also, make an extra set of each pair of tracks to serve as patterns for next time.

Getting Started

If possible, try to collect some actual animal tracks. Mix two parts plaster of paris with one part water. Pour the mix on prints you find in the mud, sand, or snow. When the plaster is dry, just pull it away from the ground, brush off, and add to your center! Display a basket of books that show pictures of animals and their tracks (see page 32 for samples). Invite children to share track molds they might have at home.

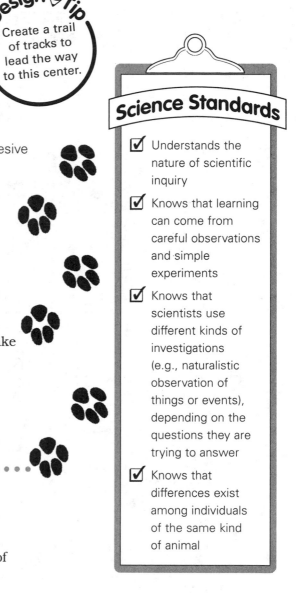

Science Standards

- ☑ Understands the nature of scientific inquiry
- ☑ Knows that learning can come from careful observations and simple experiments
- ☑ Knows that scientists use different kinds of investigations (e.g., naturalistic observation of things or events), depending on the questions they are trying to answer
- ☑ Knows that differences exist among individuals of the same kind of animal

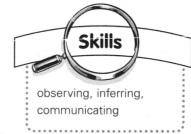

Skills

observing, inferring, communicating

Introducing the Center

Ask students what kinds of discoveries they think they might make at the new center. Encourage them to look for clues (the animal-track trail leading to the center). Can they guess what kinds of animals left these tracks? Record their guesses. As they work at the center and learn more about the tracks, they can circle correct guesses.

Activity #1

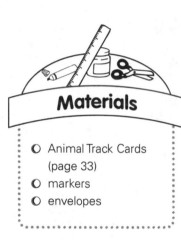

Materials

- Animal Track Cards (page 33)
- markers
- envelopes

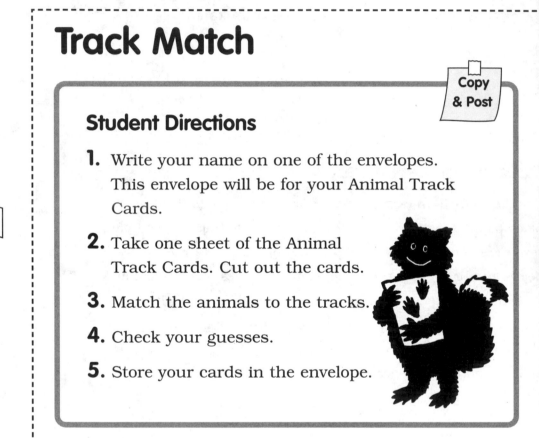

Track Match

Copy & Post

Student Directions

1. Write your name on one of the envelopes. This envelope will be for your Animal Track Cards.

2. Take one sheet of the Animal Track Cards. Cut out the cards.

3. Match the animals to the tracks.

4. Check your guesses.

5. Store your cards in the envelope.

Teaching Tip

To create an answer key, make a couple of extra copies of the reproducible. Cut apart the cards and match the animals to the tracks. Paste these pairs together on a separate sheet of paper. Label and laminate.

Extension

Students can use their animal-track cards to play a matching game. Have them team up, shuffle one set of cards, arrange them facedown, and take turns trying to turn over a matching set.

Teaching Tip

Make the stencils ahead of time. Copy the animal tracks below and paste to old file folders. Cut the tracks apart. For life-size tracks, enlarge when copying.

Making Tracks

Copy & Post

Student Directions

1. Trace track stencils onto file folders.

2. Color in the track shapes. Cut it out.

3. Use your stencils to make a track design.

Materials

- ○ animal track stencils
- ○ copy paper
- ○ markers
- ○ old file folders (cut into various sizes for children to use to make their own track stencils)

Extension

Encourage students to make new track stencils to share (other than the ones pictured). They can get ideas from animal-track books in the center. Students might make track trivia cards—showing the tracks on one side and the animal on the other.

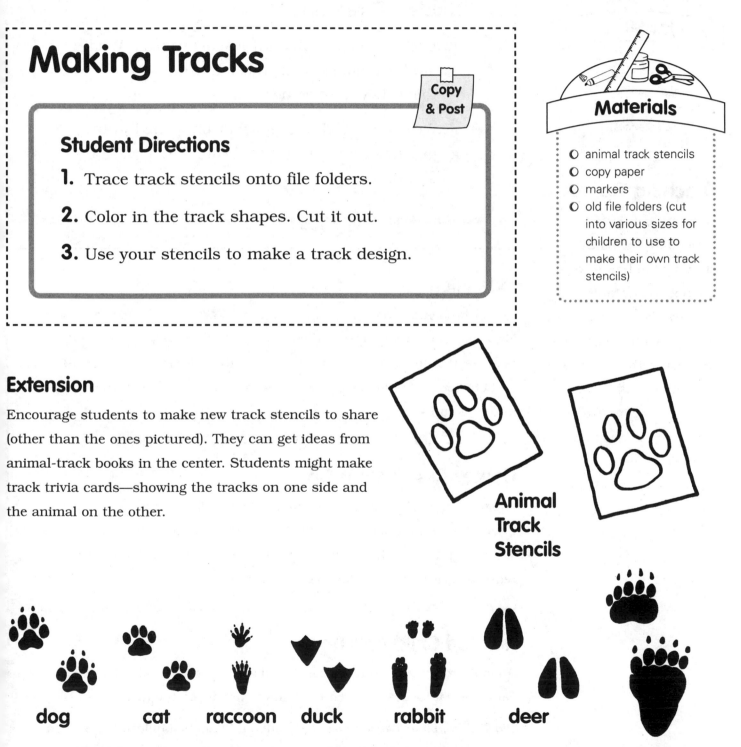

Animal Track Stencils

dog   cat   raccoon   duck   rabbit   deer

bear

Activity #3

Track Tales

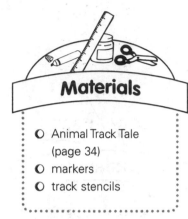

Copy & Post

Student Directions

1. Look at the picture on the activity sheet. What kind of animals made these tracks? What do you think they were doing?

2. Write a story that tells what happened in this picture. You may work by yourself or with a friend.

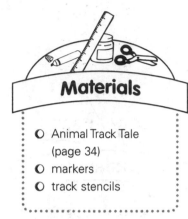

Materials

- ○ Animal Track Tale (page 34)
- ○ markers
- ○ track stencils

Teaching Tip

Give students some options for telling their stories. Children who are not comfortable with writing a story independently might team up with a student who is. Students might also read their stories into a tape recorder or rehearse their stories at the center, then share an oral reading with the class.

Extension

If your students show a lot of interest in this activity, provide them with large sheets of chart paper and encourage them to create their own track pictures that tell stories. Invite children to display their stories at the center and challenge classmates to find clues that might tell them what happened in the pictures.

Center Assessment Tip

As students work through the center activities, observe whether they understand that different animals make different kinds of tracks. Check to see if they can match animals to tracks. See if they are able to form reasonable explanations for tracks pictured.

Related Children's Books

Animal Tracks by Arthur Dorros (Scholastic, 1991). This book's guessing-game format invites children to identify animals by their tracks.

Big Tracks, Little Tracks: Following Animal Prints by Millicent E. Selsam (HarperTrophy, 1999). Wonderful illustrations teach children how to track animals by finding footprints and other clues.

Animal Track Cards

's Animal Track Tale

Name _____

The Outer-Space Station

The moon and stars may be far away, but the activities in this center give students a chance to experience some of the wonders of these celestial bodies. Upon entering the outer-space station, your young astronauts will identify several constellations and record the ever-changing shape of the moon.

Materials

- black craft paper
- white chalk
- foil stars or star stickers
- construction paper
- glitter paints and brushes
- stapler

Decorating the Center

Cover the board with the black paper. Use the white chalk to draw the outline of a few favorite constellations onto the night sky. Position the stars on the sky to indicate correctly the stars' places in the constellations. Invite students to add more constellations to the display. Label each constellation, as well as individual stars. Add a construction-paper frame to your display and use glitter paint to make knobs and dials that suggest you are peering through a space-station window. Have students make glitter-decorated construction-paper stars. Dangle from a ceiling wire.

Introducing the Center

Generate interest in this center by asking students what they would need to wear if they were visiting outer space. Ask students how space suits help protect astronauts, for example by shielding them from extreme temperatures. Next, have students work in groups of four to create astronaut cutouts. Give each group a large piece of white paper. Have one volunteer from each group lie down on the paper while others in the group trace the outline. Invite students to design a spacesuit around the outline. Display the astronauts in the center.

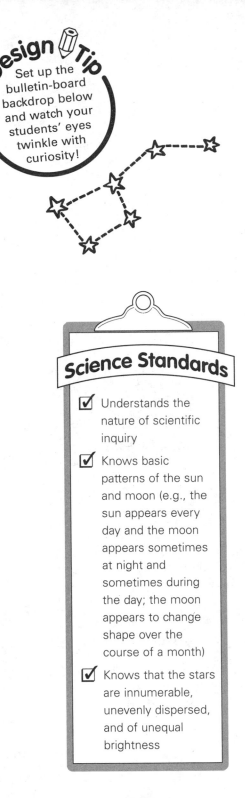

Science Standards

- ☑ Understands the nature of scientific inquiry
- ☑ Knows basic patterns of the sun and moon (e.g., the sun appears every day and the moon appears sometimes at night and sometimes during the day; the moon appears to change shape over the course of a month)
- ☑ Knows that the stars are innumerable, unevenly dispersed, and of unequal brightness

Skills

observing, predicting, collecting and recording data

Getting Started

Put together a moon journal that will travel back and forth with students. Assign one student per night to observe the moon, record findings in the notebook that night, then copy to the class calendar the next morning. Encourage all students to look for the moon each night. Sometimes the moon may not be visible because of cloud cover, a late rising time, or a new moon. So that you are sure to have an illustration of the moon for every day of the month (or at least most days), be prepared to fill in the calendar (by consulting an almanac or daily newspaper).

Activity #1

Materials

◐ Moon Watcher*
   (page 39)
◐ wall-size calendar

*Note: If you start this activity in the middle of the month, just have children note months and dates accordingly.

Moon Watch

Copy & Post

Student Directions

1. On your Moon Watcher activity sheet, draw the different ways you've seen the moon look.

2. Check the Moon Watcher calendar in the center every day. Fill in your calendar to show what the moon looks like each night.

3. After the calendar is filled in, finish the Moon Watcher worksheet.

Teaching Tip

Make the Moon Watcher calendar a permanent feature in your science center. This will go a long way in helping children recognize the pattern of the moon phases.

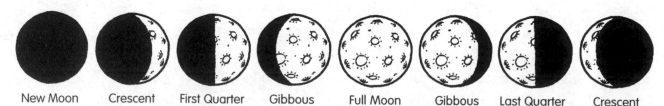

New Moon · Crescent · First Quarter · Gibbous · Full Moon · Gibbous · Last Quarter · Crescent

Activity #2

Constellation Creations

Student Directions

Copy & Post

1. Look at one of the constellation cards.

2. Count how many stars are in the constellation. Take this many stars from the box.

3. Arrange the stars to match the constellation on the card.

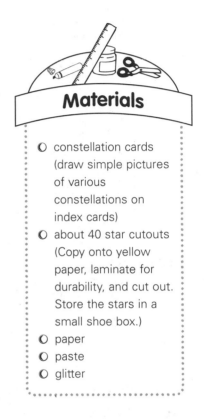

4. Try making the constellations found on the other cards.

5. Make your own constellation. Place the stars on a piece of paper. Trace around each star. Connect the stars so they make a picture. Give your constellation a name.

6. Put a dab of paste on each star in your constellation. Sprinkle with glitter.

Materials

- constellation cards (draw simple pictures of various constellations on index cards)
- about 40 star cutouts (Copy onto yellow paper, laminate for durability, and cut out. Store the stars in a small shoe box.)
- paper
- paste
- glitter

Activity #3

Starry Stories

Getting Started

Create a "Starry Stories" audiotape by taping stories about constellations and how they came to be. *Star Tales* by Gretchen Will Mayo (Walker, 1988) is a good source for stories. Make a simple picture of each constellation included in the audiotape story. Laminate these pictures and staple together to make a book for students to use while listening to the tape.

Activity #3

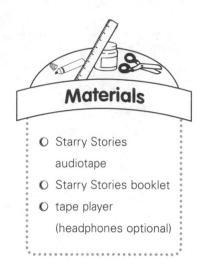

Materials

- Starry Stories audiotape
- Starry Stories booklet
- tape player (headphones optional)

Starry Stories

Copy & Post

Student Directions

1. Put the Starry Stories tape in the tape player.

2. Start the tape.

3. Look at the Starry Stories book while you listen to the tape. Do you recognize some constellations?

Follow-up

After listening to these stories, students can make up their own stories about the constellations they created in Activity 2. Let students record their stories on tape, making a "Starry Stories, Volume 2"!

Center Assessment Tip

At the conclusion of this center, hold a space-station celebration. Students can create star-shaped invitations. Let students take guests on guided tours, sharing their constellation creations and recorded stories. Serve small round cookies or crackers and ask students to bite away at their cookies so they look like different phases of the moon. Don't forget to have some Milky Way juice (milk) on hand to wash down the moons!

Related Children's Books

The Magic Schoolbus Lost in the Solar System by Joanna Cole (Scholastic, 1990). Ms. Frizzle's class takes a tour of space.

The Moon Book by Gail Gibbons (Holiday House, 1998). A kid-friendly overview of our planet's closest neighbor.

So That's How the Moon Changes Shape by Allan Fowle (Children's Press, 1991). Simple text and photographs will help young children understand the phases of the moon.

Find the Constellations by H. A. Rey (Houghton Mifflin, 1976). A wonderful guide for young stargazers from the creator of Curious George.

Name _____

Moon Watcher

Keep a moon watch calendar. First write in the days and dates. Next find out what the moon looks like each night of the month. Draw the moon for each date. Look at the pictures of the moon's phases around the calendar. Write the name of the phase under each picture you draw.

Sunday	Monday	Tuesday	Wednesday	Thursday	Friday	Saturday

Write a sentence that tells something you learned about the moon.

_____

_____

_____

Water Wonders

Water comes in many shapes and forms. At this center, students will explore properties of water and observe how water molecules like to stick together, demonstrating cohesion and surface tension.

Design Tip
Use an old umbrella to "wet" students' appetites for some drippy fun.

Materials

- blue cellophane
- scissors
- umbrellas
- packing tape
- heavy white paper
- water-based markers
- paintbrush
- water

Decorating the Center

Cut cellophane into streamers each at least 3 feet long and 1 to 2 inches wide. Tape the streamers to the underside edge of an open umbrella. Hook the umbrella handle over a ceiling wire so the water streamers appear to drip out of the open umbrella. Secure the handle to the wire so it cannot fall. Surround the umbrella with the water drops described in "Introducing the Center."

· ·

Getting Started

Plan on setting up at least one water-related Window Watch activity (see Center 4, page 26) while you have this center running. If you haven't already set up an aquarium in your classroom, now is the time to do it. Guppies are low-maintenance, inexpensive fish. Or try raising tadpoles or providing a temporary habitat for an adult frog.

· ·

Introducing the Center

Have students cut out large water drops from heavy white paper. Have students write words that complete the phrase "*Water is…*" on the paper drops with water-based markers. Demonstrate how to brush the entire drop using water then have students do the same. Hang students' water drops above the center.

Activity #1

How Many Drops?

Copy & Post

Student Directions

1. How many drops fit on the heads side of a penny? Record your guess in your Water Log (#1).

2. Fill an eyedropper with water.

3. Count the number of drops you can put on the penny before the water falls off the penny. Record this number in your log (#1).

4. Flip the penny over to the tails side. Repeat steps 1 to 3 (#2).

5. Which side held more drops? (#3)

Materials

- eyedroppers
- plastic cups for water
- pennies
- Water Log (page 43)

Extension

Many students will probably want to try different water-dropping techniques, experiment with other pennies, and so on. Support this exploration of variables to enhance students' understanding of the watery concepts of cohesion and surface tension.

Activity #2

Evaporation Sensations

Copy & Post

Student Directions

1. Dip a sponge in the dish of water. Squeeze water out of the sponge back into the dish.

2. Make a wet spot on the blackboard with the sponge.

3. Record what happens to the wet spot (#4).

4. Now paint a mini picture with the watercolors (#5). Be sure to sign your painting!

Materials

- small sponge pieces (2 by 2 inches)
- shallow dish of water
- small blackboards (lap- or easel-size)
- watercolor paints and brushes
- Water Log (page 43)

Follow-up

As students observe the wet spots dry, or evaporate, challenge them to think of ways they could make the spot dry more quickly (such as blowing on it).

Getting Started

Enlist students' help in mixing red water in one cup and blue water in another.

Purple Puddles

Copy & Post

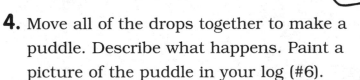

Student Directions

1. Get a tray. Put one drop of blue water and one drop of red water on the tray.

2. Use a straw to move one of the drops toward the other. What happens when the two drops are close to each other?

3. Put more blue drops and more red drops on the tray.

4. Move all of the drops together to make a puddle. Describe what happens. Paint a picture of the puddle in your log (#6).

Materials

- foam food trays
- plastic cups for water
- eyedroppers
- red and blue food coloring
- straws
- Water Log (page 43)

Center Assessment Tip

Repeat the activity in "Introducing the Center" (page 40). Compare the way students complete the phrase "*Water is...*" now that they have worked through the center activities.

• •

Related Children's Books

A Drop of Water: A Book of Science and Wonder by Walter Wick (Scholastic, 1998). Close-up photographs of water in its different forms teach kids about the water cycle, surface tension, and more.

The Science Book of Water by Neil Ardley (Harcourt, 1992). A handy source of simple experiments.

_____ 's

Water Log

1. How many drops fit on the heads side of a penny?

   My guess _____   My count _____

2. How many drops fit on the tails side?

   My guess _____   My count _____

3. Which side holds more drops? _____

4. This is what happened to the wet spot.

5. My mini watercolor:

6. This is the way I made my puddle.

The Recycling Center

Design Tip
Recycle simple cardboard boxes as a reminder to protect the planet.

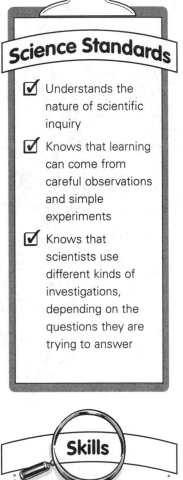

Reduce. Reuse. Recycle. These will become more than words for your students after they have worked at this Recycling Center! Students will get involved in the actual recycling process: classifying different plastics, reusing some paper and rubber products, and reducing waste.

Materials

- ○ glue
- ○ markers
- ○ pieces of discarded cardboard
- ○ boxes for sorting trash
- ○ trash samples for each of the sorting categories you will include

Decorating the Center

Use markers to draw trash cans on the boxes. Label the cardboard pieces to create a sign for each box. Attach the signs to the wall behind the boxes. Glue real trash samples to each sign.

Getting Started

Start making plans for this center several weeks ahead of time. Send a note home asking families to save some of the following items:

- **plastics** such as milk jugs, foam food trays, yogurt cups and lids (request that these be cleaned before being sent to school)
- **paper** including old maps and magazines with some full-page color pictures

Locate an old rubber inner tube for Activity 2. Check with a local bicycle repair shop or garage. Make a sign for the Recycling Center. You might consider having a contest for the sign design. Let students vote on their favorite design. Then let the winner make the sign.

Introducing the Center

Discuss what recycling means. Invite students to share their own efforts to recycle. Introduce the terms *reuse* and *reduce.* Brainstorm ways recycling and reusing help reduce waste and conserve natural resources. Hold a ribbon-cutting ceremony to announce the opening of your class Recycling Center.

Activity #1

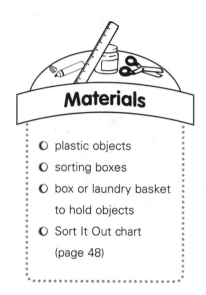

Materials

- plastic objects
- sorting boxes
- box or laundry basket to hold objects
- Sort It Out chart (page 48)

Sort It Out

Student Directions

Copy & Post

1. How are the plastic containers the same? How are they different?

2. Think of a way to sort the plastic containers. Use the boxes to sort them.

3. Count how many objects are in each box. Write the numbers on the activity sheet.

4. Tell how the plastics in each box are alike.

Teaching Tip

If you have space limitations and are unable to have children work with actual plastic containers, just cut pictures of plastics from magazines. Use shoe-box lids as sorting bins.

Extension

Have students investigate where plastics in their community go (to a landfill or a recycling center?). Make plans to recycle as many of the objects as possible at the end of the center.

Recycled Bicycle

Student Directions

Copy & Post

1. Draw one or two interesting shapes on a piece of inner tube.

2. Cut out the shapes. Glue to a piece of wood. Let dry.

3. Press the rubber part of the stamp in the ink pad. Stamp a design on a sheet of paper.

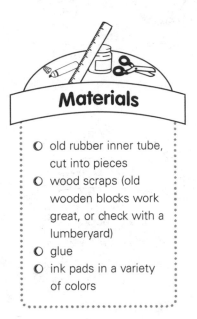

Materials

○ old rubber inner tube, cut into pieces
○ wood scraps (old wooden blocks work great, or check with a lumberyard)
○ glue
○ ink pads in a variety of colors

Extension

Place the student-made stamp collection in a shoe box and add to the center. Make a set of pattern cards using students' stamps. Students can revisit the center to figure out the next stamp in the sequence and continue the pattern. Encourage students to make their own sequenced pattern cards. Or cover an entire wall of the center with butcher paper. Turn students loose with their stamps to create wallpaper prints.

The Envelope, Please

Copy & Post

Student Directions

1. Choose a picture or map.

2. Turn the picture facedown on the table.

3. Put the envelope pattern on the picture.

4. Trace around the pattern. Mark the fold lines.

5. Put paste on the sides. Fold up on fold line 2.

6. Fold down on fold line 1.

PICTURE ON THE BOTTOM SIDE

PASTE

FOLD 1

FOLD 2

ENVELOPE PATTERN

Materials

○ pages from old magazines (select pages that are colorful or have interesting pictures

○ old maps (cut to 8 1/2 by 11 inches)

○ envelope pattern (see sample, left)

Teaching Tip

Enlarge illustrations of the steps and display at the center to assist students as they complete Activity 3.

Center Assessment Tip

Make a student-produced recycling flier to share with families. Have each student contribute an idea about recycling for the flier. (Remember to copy fliers onto recycled paper!)

Related Children's Books

Recycle! A Handbook for Kids by Gail Gibbons (Little Brown, 1996). Learn how paper, aluminum cans, plastics, and polystyrene can be transformed from trash into useful products.

Compost Critters by Bianca Lavies (Dutton, 1993). Text and photographs teach a lively ecology lesson about earth's recyclers—millipedes, mites, earthworms, and other busy critters.

The White Bicycle by Rob Lewis (Farrar, Straus & Giroux, 1988). A bike is passed along through a series of owners.

Name _____

Sort It Out

	How Many?	Ways the Containers in Each Box Are Alike
Box 1		
Box 2		
Box 3		
Box 4		